THE FÜHRER BUNKER

Also by W. D. Snodgrass

POETRY
Heart's Needle, Alfred A. Knopf, 1959.
After Experience, Harper & Row, Publishers, 1968.

TRANSLATIONS
Gallows Songs by Christian Morgenstern (with Lore Segal)
The University of Michigan Press, 1967.
Six Troubadour Songs (with music), Burning Deck, 1977.
Traditional Hungarian Songs (with music), Charles Seluzicki, 1977.

PROSE
In Radical Pursuit: Critical Essays and Lectures, Harper & Row,
Publishers, 1975.

THE FÜHRER BUNKER

A CYCLE OF POEMS IN PROGRESS

W.D. SNODGRASS

BOA EDITIONS • BROCKPORT N. Y. • 1977

I am indebted to the Guggenheim Foundation for a fellowship to research this project
and to the Corporation of Yaddo for a period of residence for concentrated writing.

I cannot begin to name all the others who have helped me. Former Minister Albert Speer
granted me a most provocative interview and Herr Herbert Graf of the U.S.I.S. clarified
many problems for me. Friends and fellow poets have encouraged me and supplied in-
formation or criticism: Donald Hall, James Merrill, Gary Miranda, Keith and Rosmarie
Waldrop, William Heyen and Lore Segal. Anyone familiar with Henri Coulette's *The War
of the Secret Agents* will see my indebtedness to it. Once again, I am most grateful to
that lady to whom I dedicate this book.

-- W. D. Snodgrass

Grateful acknowledgment is made to *The American Poetry Review, The Georgia Review*
and *Seneca Review* in which some of these poems first appeared.
Lyrics from "Tea for Two" by Irving Caesar. Copyright © 1924 Warner Bros. Inc. Copy-
right renewed. All rights reserved. Used by permission.

Typeset in Primer Roman by Advertising and Marketing Graphics, Rochester, N.Y.
Printed on Mohawk Superfine Text
Binding by Gene Eckert Inc., Rochester, N.Y.
Printed at the Visual Studies Workshop, Rochester, N.Y.
Joan Lyons, Design and production co-ordinator

Library of Congress Cataloging in Publication Number 77-074040

ISBN 0-918526-00-0 Cloth
     0-918526-01-9 Paper

First Edition: June, 1977
Second Printing April 1978

for Camille

THE FÜHRER BUNKER

(1 April - 1 May, 1945)

VOICES

THE FÜHRER BUNKER

ADOLF HITLER

-- 1 April, 1945.

*(Easter Sunday and April Fool's
Day. Hitler sits alone in his con-
ference room looking at the large
map of Europe on the wall.)*

Down: I got it all. Almost.
Brat; fed sick on sugartits.
Shreds, chunks, chewed-over
Races. It rises up again.
Say I spoiled my appetite.

(turns to the situation reports on his table)

Heidelberg, Danzig, practically undamaged;
Gone over; surrendered. Half a million
Squirm out of our glory. Our best troops
Sacked up in the Ruhr. Too gutless
Even to get killed.

(takes a report from the table)

And Speer
Still lies. Will not raze his factories,
The bridges, mines. He'd let these ditch-worms
Go on spawning, spawning. So yesterday
I gave Speer back his offices. Truly, truly,
You regret how kind you've been.

Always this soft side mounting up;
My mother's cake-and-candy-boy.
She and I, we let him off -- Alois,
My own half-brother -- let him
Clear out of the house to England;
Let him back here in Berlin
Where just to shut that mouth
Made rumors.

(another report)

Our enemies at Easter Mass. Sick, sniveling,
Forgiving Jesus of these Christians.

With her, it was all my way.
Talk; talk to her. Her thoughts lay
Open. My voice soaked into her,
All sides, like a showerspray. She
Rammed it down the old man's throat.

Sniff them; track them; let them slither out.
Strasser, my brother in the Party. His brother.
Schleicher, Von Papen. My own worst enemy.
Each triumph filled the dark with whispering:
My mercies gather against me; a defeat; death.

The day they buried her, I thought
Time now; time. I cannot live
The mercies I mean to. No choice:
When did *I* choose I should die?

Ernst Roehm, finally. By then, I knew
Better. Still this vile kindheartedness let him
Weasel out to South America. Once come back
Here to Berlin, though, he dared stand against me,
My brother-in-arms, my old comrade Ernst,

I feel already this ground
Swallow me. I so shall
Swallow all this ground
Till we two are one flesh.

We hacked them down like sewer rats --
Traitors, unreliables, all who learned
Too much, who thwarted us; dropped them
Into ditches, rivers, drop and rot there.

That first time, I could believe
I move among the Powers once more.
Our President's praised my gallantry.
Faced by my firing squads, men raise
Proud arms to heil me. The crime
I choose is God's law. My lie, Truth.

(background sounds: the Nuremberg Rallies)

From ten million speakers, my voice
Falls like the farmers' rain; sing, sing
My name. Past evil, time or consequence,
My nerves clang with the iron worlds.

(sits down at the table)

Too late. The Powers move on.
After our first putsch failed,
This left arm shaking, pinned down
By the right. Since Stalingrad, this
Shivering I can't control.

Who else sold out? Bremen? Magdeburg?
They would go on in this pisswallow, in
Disgrace, shame. Who could we send to make
Their lives worth less to them? In our camps,
You gas them, shoot, club, strangle them,
Tramp them down into trenches, thick as leaves.
Out of the ground, at night, they squirm up
Through the tangled bodies, crawl off in the woods.
Every side now, traitors, our deserters, native
Populations, they rise up like vomit, flies
Out of bad meat, sewers backing up. Up
There, now, in the bombed-out gardens,
That sickly, faint film coming over
The trees again, along the shattered branches
Buds festering. In shell-holes, trash heaps,
Some few green leaves, grass spikes thrust
Up through the ashes, through the cracked cement,
Shove up into the light again.

(returns to the table and begins drawing up directives)

Well,
We may dream them up an Easter
Fool's gift yet. Decorate a few
More street lamps. Something
To look up to. Then order out
Those few troops still up North.
Stalin: count on him to clean house.
Boots, bones, buckles -- nothing
Sticks in that man's craw.

(rises)

So; we must go out now. Suppose
My diet cook could be awake yet? Suppose
We could still find a little chocolate cake?
A little schlag, perhaps?

ALBERT SPEER

-- 18 April, 1945.

(Hitler's architect, friend, and finally Armaments Minister, Speer tried to tell him of the nation's real state and also countered many of his destructive orders. Here, he comes to ask Hitler not to defend Berlin against the Russian attack, which began two days earlier. Before going down the bunker steps, he pauses in the Chancellery.)

Paul,
My old
Schoolmate,
My own doctor --
Last week I was there.
Propped in his armchair;
No nurse. The needle, used,
By his armrest. Talking, smoking;
Our most acute diagnostic mind. What
He would have seen at one glance in his
Patients, he can explain away, can talk it all
To death. He neglects his knowing.

He who
Once told
Us all how
He would die by
Cancer, describes
All this once more now.
And he sees nothing. Well,
He may escape the guns, escape
Acknowledging what it is his cells
Have been preparing, step by step, in darkness,
Past all control.

Down
There, they
Will be talking
Strategies, horoscopes,
Talking "miracles." While he,
Dry spit on his lips, the left arm
Paralyzed, will lurch up off the table
Shaking worn-out maps, quoting the latest
Falsified intelligence, assigning forces wiped out
Weeks ago, doling out supplies we never had, shrieking
At the helpless generals for traitors, ruthless counter-thrusts,
Shrieking for revenge.

As
For me,
I will be
Talking, asking
Him to spare this city --
Meaning let this city fall --
Assuring him I have obeyed his decrees,
Scorched this earth of all that could support
An enemy. That could support our people. I should
Have asked myself whether I'll come back up these steps
Alive. Or, maybe, better not
To know. Better not.

DR. JOSEPH GOEBBELS

-- 19 April, 1945.

(The Propaganda Chief, slightly crippled since childhood, had many love affairs, especially with actresses. On this date, he was at his home on Schwanenwerder, Wannsee, Berlin. Planning to move to the bunker to die, he sent away his aged mother, whose firm faith he always admired and envied. In his study, he empties papers from his desk into the fireplace.)

East Prussia, Silesia, Norway --
We're getting good at loss. Today,
My country house fell. Soon, we'll be
Preaching desert philosophy.

BERLIN'S DEFENDER
STRIPS FOR ACTION

Mementos. Who ever would have thought
I'd own so much? Still, you get caught
Wanting things.

(takes a packet of letters)

Anka -- my first lover.
I pissed away months, moping over
That fool.

(drops them in the fire)

Elsa -- she called me "Stropp."
But that time I came out on top
And dropped her first.

(drops these, then many others, in the fire)

The trash! You get
Possessed with ownership.

Give all thy worldly goods
unto the poor and follow me

16

And yet
My foot spared me the worst excess.
You learn that you can live on less
When you can't grow. You can still change
Your shape, your loyalties; estrange
Your past -- friends, family, lover,
Heroes, beliefs.

(picks up the photograph of a beautiful woman)

Lida Baarova.
Lida Baarova.

(puts it back; takes other papers)

What a loss
To us -- Gregor Strasser, my old boss.
And Ernst Roehm. You can't help make friends.
Things you'll just have to turn against.

NAZIS DUMP STRASSER
ESCAPES TO ITALY

(burns these; takes others)

Actresses -- they live to change roles.
You don't ask them to pledge their souls
To one part. So, they come; they go.
There's no one there you'd care to know.

(takes Baarova's picture again)

Baarova. Liduschka. There
Is one beautiful woman. You'd care
Where she's gone. If you knew. We kept clear
One phone line, so each of us could hear
The other breathe. When he forbid
Us to each other . . . I really did
Think I could be faithful. Desire
Deludes a man.

(tears the picture across)

So. In the fire.
But after things like that, you want.
You try suits, women, cars; you haunt
The nightclubs and the theatre;

17

NAZI WHORELORD
COUNTS CONQUESTS

You buy up paintings, furniture,
Plates, silver, glass. You can't help start
Hankering to keep some small part
Of this world. You wear satins, ermine,
Rouge and rings, gross as Fat Hermann.

Behold a camel shall
more easily pass . . .

*(goes to the French window and looks
out at the lights of Berlin burning)*

Now we can get down to what
Counts -- cleaning out the whole vile lot.
Ernst Roehm was right: only a man
Who has no possessions can
Afford ideals. We learn once more
To do without. Where but in war --
The leveler -- do all things meet?
Rich and poor, now, dig in the street
Together; walls bombed out, in flame,
Bury weak men and strong the same.

The race is not to the swift
nor the battle to the strong

DESTRUCTION PASSES
ALL PREVIOUS BOUNDS

Each Ami bomb, each Russian shell
Helps us to clear away this Hell
Of Europe, mankind as it was.
These fools only further our cause:
A cleared road out of this unjust
World, a world of lies, pandering, lust,
Deformity. This is to be
Young again -- idealistic, free.

(goes to the piano)

EDUCATION MINISTER
PLAYS GERMAN SONGS

(plays and sings)

We've got to go off to the wars,
    And who knows when, my brothers?
We march out through the gates of town --
    Farewell, both Father and Mother.

Dear God, why are the heavens glowing
    Rose-red as burning coals?
It is the blood of soldiers flowing.
    Lord have mercy on our souls.

Farewell, both Father and Mother. Today
I sent my poor old mother away.

(takes her picture from the piano)

FAREWELL TO THE PEASANT MOTHER
WHOSE SIMPLE FAITH INSPIRED HIM

Old and poor? Yes. As sure and steady
As she ever was. And ready
For what comes. Neither one would let
Me give them one red cent. Yet, yet
They scratched and scrimped years, just to get
My first piano. So I could
Have something. Almost as good.

It was your clear faith that drove me through the world. But I had the Midas touch. In my fingers everything turned smoke -- beliefs, creeds, faiths.

Now I have sent you away, too. You never reproached me, though you must have wondered at the life we led.

Go. Take the time that's left you. It is right; you can believe. I doubt. I doubt.

> #### Leave both father and
> #### mother and follow after me

*(breaks her picture and throws it
  in the fire)*

19

Ho! Clubfoot Joe, the Boche warlord
Comfortably seated at the keyboard;
Your Emperor Zero now returns
To tickle the keys while Berlin burns.

(plays and sings again)

Within my father's garden,
  Two little saplings grow;
The one of them bears nutmegs,
  The other one bears cloves.

The nutmeg's fresh and lovely;
  The cloves are sharp and sweet.
Now comes the time of parting
  Never again to meet.

The winter's snows are melting;
  Far off these streams will flow.
Now out of my sight you vanish;
  Out of my thoughts you go.

(gets up)

Out of sight, out of mind. We're purer,
Rid of her. What's left now? My Führer,
My used wife, the daughters, and one
Partially retarded son.
Flimsy enough, these ties of mine.
Tonight, we break off one more line
That lashed us to this pit of violence.

(closes the piano)

No more songs. We must practice silence.

MAGDA GOEBBELS

-- 19 April, 1945.

*(Planning to destroy first her six
children by Goebbels, then herself,
Magda prepares to move to the
bunker.)*

i

How can you do the things you know you'll do? --
One last act to bring back integrity.
I've got just one desire left: to be true.

You can't pick how you'll live. Our times will screw
Your poor last virtues from you, ruthlessly.
How can you do the things you know you'll do?

My mother drove me on: get married to
Quandt. Rich. Kind enough. If elderly.
I've got just one desire left: to be true.

He turned me against Friedlander, the Jew --
My stepfather who'd raised me lovingly.
How can you do the things you know you'll do?

Quandt trapped me with young Ernst. He planned to sue
Till I found his old tax books. And the key.
I've got just one desire left: to be true.

Those thin books brought me in the revenue
For leisure, for the best society.
How can you do the things you know you'll do?

And then I heard Him speak: our Leader, who
Might have been talking to no one but me.
I've got just one desire left: to be true
Till death to Him. And what I know I'll do.

How can you live through what life brings you to?
Who's showed us, ever, the least loyalty?
All of us find it hard just to be true.

The Chief was wild for me; yet we all knew
He couldn't marry -- He needs to be free.
How can you live through what life brings you to?

They said why not take Joseph, then; *in lieu*,
The Chief would visit our place secretly.
All of us find it hard just to be true.

Joseph said *he'd* play false. But he came through;
He kept that single promise faithfully.
How can you live through what life brings you to?

I, too, found lovers, given time. Some few
Were his good friends -- his staff, his ministry.
All of us find it hard just to be true.

He wanted Lida; I took Karl. Then who
But the Chief sealed us shut -- a family!
How can you live through what life brings you to?

So now I won't leave Joseph; I'll die, too.
The children? They'll just have to come with me.
All of us find it hard just to be true
Till death to all this false world brings you to.

iii

The children? They'll just have to come with me.
At their age, how could they find their own way?
We must preserve them from disloyalty.

They're too good for the world we all foresee.
If they were old enough, we know they'd say
It's right and just they'll have to come with me.

My father left -- divorced -- when I was three
So how could I leave them alone today?
We must preserve them from disloyalty.

They've been the fist behind my policy
Since Joseph and that Slav girl ran astray;
It's right and just they'll have to come with me.

I slammed his door on him. "Of course you're free.
It's time they learned who cares and who'll betray."
We must preserve them from disloyalty.

My father came; he said Joseph would be
Ruin to us all. I turned him away.
It's right and just they'll have to come with me.

He begged to visit them. He will not see
Them till he dies. That's just the price he'll pay.
We must preserve them from disloyalty
And this false world. They'll have to come with me.

iv

You try to spare them the worst misery;
Who knows what cold force they'd be subject to?
How could we let them fall to treachery,

Disgrace, to brute foes? At the best, they'd see
Scorn in the face of every Red or Jew.
You try to spare them the worst misery.

In evil days, models of constancy
Are the one thing that will still see men through.
How could we let them fall to treachery

When they've once known our Leader? Yet if He,
If we go, just how many could stay true?
You try to spare them the worst misery

Of wanting this, that. From our own past, we
Know things they might have to say or do.
How could we let them fall to treachery,

To making base terms with an enemy,
Denying us and our best ideals, too?
You try to spare them the worst misery

But they'd still want to live. What if they'd be
Happy -- they could prove all we thought untrue.
How could we let them fall to treachery
And their own faults? You end their misery.

COL. GEN. GOTTHARD HEINRICI
COMMANDER, ARMY GROUP VISTULA

-- 19 April, 1945.

(Replacing Himmler, Heinrici com-
manded the forces in the North and
East. He resisted taking Berlin under
his command and evaded Hitler's
more destructive orders. Here, he
leaves the bunker for his head-
quarters at Birkenhain. By now the
Russians are across the Oder and
30 miles from Berlin.)

Army Group Vistula? Ghosts. The ghost
Of ghosts. Some fairy story dreamed up
Only after the Vistula had been lost.
Defend Berlin? In Moscow's outskirts
I started that two years ago. Now'days,
We're losing on the Oder. The ridge
At Seelow, taken: our East gate's open.
And Konev's tanks close in from the South.
I am to commit our best remaining unit,
Weidling's 56th Corps, under sentence to
Stand fast or die? The better part
Already have been killed for us
Twice over. If only nothing but Berlin
Were indefensible! Once; once --
That's enough to die.

ADOLF HITLER

-- 20 April, 1945; 1900 hours.

(After his birthday ceremony, Hitler has withdrawn to his sitting room where he sits with one of Blondi's puppies on his knee. Earlier in the day he had gone up into the garden for the last time.)

Better stuffed in a bag; drowned.
My best bitch pregnant once she can't
Survive.

The man will lie down on his back; his partner crouches over his head
or chest as he prefers.

My Effie's little sister
Knocked up by Fegelein. My luck
Lets me off one humiliation:
I breed no child.

He, of course, is completely naked.

This mockery:
Pisspot generals whining for surrender;
Party maggots bringing presents;
Careful not to wish me a long life --
Their one failure I can share.
Pulling at me, whimpering for
Their cities, populations, lives.

Sometimes, she may remove only her underthings. The private parts,
suddenly exposed, can provide an exquisite shock and pleasure.

Cub, in Landsberg Prison, after
Our first putsch failed, my flowers
Filled three prison rooms. The faithful
Sang beside me in my cell.
I unwrapped presents, cut my cake. We
Laughed: where was the file inside?

The cake my mother made me . . . No . . .

Usually she will turn her back.

No. That's Edmund's cake. My brother's.
But I ate Edmund's cake. I spit on
What was left.

The Prison Governor brought his family's
Kind regards. His little daughter curled up,
Like this, on my lap asleep.

She must not start at once; he must ask, even beg her, to begin.

Whimpering at me; whining. Oh,
We hear their song:

Only live. Live longer. Lead us
To the mountain fastnesses. Keep us
From the guns, the Russians . . .

"Oh stay! don't leave us here forsaken;
Our men are waiting for their führer"

In the mountains, could these shitheads be
Worthwhile? Over and over, we've said
They could survive: overcome facts.

Today I climbed two flights to the garden:
Sour smoke. Shelling. Schoolboys lined up.
Lines of graves. Hands I have to touch.

He will grovel on the floor, declaring himself unworthy to touch her
shoes, even to live.

Even the zoo animals, my good old
Neighbors, pacing their stalls till
Their keeper brings the right gift --
One lead pellet. A man who would accept
What is, is criminal, too vile to live.

It is not the mere fact of the urine or the faeces that is significant.
The crux is that he be able to watch these emerge into existence.

Suffer that again? The elevator
Locked, lurching up through dead rock
In the mountain side? Come out
Freezing, over the receding plains,
Traitorous cities, nauseous dens
And hovels, lecherous faces with insane
Beliefs, Czechs, Jews with blonde hair,
Blue eyes, who would steal our birthright,
Pull us down into putrescence, slime?

Edmund died though, my brother,
When I was eleven. His birthday
Would have been some days ago.

She must now show disgust; may revile him, even kick at him.

She lost three others. She, only
She, was glad I had survived.

Only when he is fully excited by his own demands, may she release
her urine, open her bowels. The danger of taking this matter in his
mouth heightens the excitement.

Only live; live longer. Don't
Leave us to the loneliness,
The spoiling of affections.

He kept me in. But she,
She made a special cake for me --
Only the two of us together.

Now he will probably achieve his climax, alone and without assis-
tance.

Namesake, cub, you've done your month
In this filth. My cake; I'll eat it, too.

The First War soldiers; our Old Fighters --
That was comradeship. You have Blondi's
Underside; my diet cook, the drivers,
Secretaries -- they know how to listen.

"I stay too long; the Grail has sent for me."

28

I can eat nothing now -- only cake.
Pills and Morrell's injections.
My cake, chairs, rugs -- without them,
There's the bare concrete. Like any
Jew degenerate at Auschwitz.

When he has washed and begged forgiveness, she may embrace and
comfort him.

My birthday present, my file: my
Cartridge of pure cyanide. Crawl back
In the cave, work down in dry leaves,
An old dog deciding to lie down.

Or she may curl up by his side.

ALBERT SPEER

-- 20 April, 1945; 2200 hours.

(After Hitler's birthday ceremony,
Speer leaves the bunker, traveling
to Hamburg to subvert Hitler's
scorched earth policy. He pauses at
the top of the stairs leading out of
the bunker into the gardens.)

Take
A breath.
Your breath.
Even this air
Reeking with smoke,
With brick dust, plaster . . .
Even this darkness, this night
Sky, streaked by searchlights, flaring
With the light of our own buildings burning,
Is better than manufactured air, than man-made
Light, their talk of miracle weapons, death rays, that
Man-made darkness.

   (crosses the garden)

The
Bombers
Hold back.
An ugly sign.
The troops may be
Closing in. And the
Shelling sounds heavier:
Russian 17.5s moved up from
The Silesian front. So, the Ruhr
Gone; Silesia lost to us this last time . . .
The mines, power plants, our best installations . . .
And is that all?

   (gets into his car beside Lt. Col. von Poser;
   the car moves off through the streets of Berlin)

Today
His "birthday
Party," they come
Up to the Chancellery,
The garden, for one breath.
Shuffling along, his left foot
Dragging, patting the poor boys
Lined up there, pinning tinny medals
On their chests. Then orders them out
To be ground up under tank tread. They beam
With gratitude. He limps a little more so *they*
Will pity *him*. How long? How long?

    (the car is stopped)

What's
This now?
The Altonaer
Strasse roped off,
Burning. Could the
Lessing Strasse still
Be open?

    (the car moves on)

     Houses, whole rows,
Crushed in; frantic fire brigades
Working without water. Altendorfers,
My father's dearest friends, kept an office
There. Brick walls standing, broken masonry,
Stonework, rubble. Shadows leaping.

He has
Broken his
Word once more:
Today, the directive --
In spite of all he's said,
He will now defend this city
Street by street. Which means
He will now annihilate this city
Street by street. And lose the city
All the same. He will not see the city
Is lost, the war is lost, that we must plan
What can go on . . .

He will
Not go out
Through the towns,
Will not so much as
Look at normal casualties,
Our refugees, the photographs
That Goebbels brought him. My reports
Lie on his desk unread still, unanswered.
The officers that I brought in from Silesia,
Intelligence Heinrici sends in from the fronts,
He shrugs all this aside; he shrugs all this aside:
Irrelevant. And is that all?

At least
I tried to
Drive out to
Silesia, tried to
See. In the mines at
Rybnik, they were already
Changing over for the Russians.
At Kattowitz . . .

        Again, last night, my dreams came out
        of Käthe Kollwitz: *The Guillotine.*
        That murderous dance -- the mob was
        half-crazed, killing off its rulers.
        No doubt I must be guilty, then, of
        "bolshevistic and degenerate" dreams.
        No one confiscates and burns them.

    What was it
        Hanke saw there in the camps?
            And warned me
        not to look?
               What
    are the Russians digging up?
            The sort of thing
        I saw in the camps
            no doubt --
forced labor, wretched conditions . . .

Why let
Me live? Time
For one cigarette.
He has forbidden us all
To smoke, then sends us all
Up the chimney. Up the chimney?
Idiot. Use your eyes: if he gets his way,
We won't have a chimney standing. No doubt
He knows that I will not obey. Perhaps he knows
That I am going to betray him. And no doubt he knows
That I am faithful. That I evade my better self. That I
Neglect my knowing.

DR. JOSEPH GOEBBELS

-- 22 April, 1945.

*(On this date, Goebbels moved into
the lowest level of the bunker, taking
a room opposite Hitler's.)*

Stand back, make way, you mindless scum,
Squire Voland the Seducer's come --
Old Bock from Babelsberg whose tower
Falls silent now, whose shrunken power
For lies or lays comes hobbling home
Into this concrete catacomb.

Here's Runty Joe, the cunt collector
Who grew to greatness, first erector
Of myths and missions, fibs and fables,
Who pulled the wool then turned the tables;
He piped the tunes and called the dance
Where shirtless countries lost their pants.

Goatfooted Pan, the nation's gander
To whom Pan-Germans all played pander,
The jovial cob-swan quick to cover
Lida Baarova, his check-list lover;
Swellfoot the Tyrant, he could riddle
Men's minds away, hi-diddle-diddle.

Our little Doctor, Joe the Gimp
Comes back to limpness and his limp;
Hephaistos, Vulcan the lame smith
Whose net of lies caught one true myth:
His wife, the famous beauty, whored
By numbskull Mars, the dull warlord.

What if I took my little fling
At conquest, at adventuring,
Pried the lid of Pandora's box off --
There's nothing there to bring your rocks off.
I never saw one fucking day
So fine I courted it to stay.

If I got snarled in my own mesh
Of thighs and bellies, who wants flesh?
I never hankered after matter.
Let Hermann swell up, grosser, fatter,
Weighed down by medals, houses, clothing;
They leave me lean, secured in loathing.

As a young man, I pricked the bubble
Of every creed; I saw that rubble
And offered myself the realms of earth
Just to say Yes. But what's it worth?
No thank you, Ma'am. Behold the Ram
Of God: I doubt, therefore I am.

Here I forsake that long pricktease
Of histories, hopes, lusts, luxuries.
I come back to my first Ideal --
The vacancy that's always real.
I sniffed out all life's openings:
I loved only the holes in things

So strip down one bare cell for this
Lay Brother of the last abyss.
To me, still, all abstractions smell;
My head and nose clear in this cell
Of concrete, this confession booth
Where liars face up to blank truth.

My tongue lashed millions to the knife;
Here, I'll hold hands with my soiled wife.
My lies piped men out, hot to slaughter;
Here, I'll read stories to my daughter
Then hack off all relations, choose
Only the Nothing you can't lose,

Send back this body, fixed in its
Infantile paralysis.
I was born small; I shall grow less
Till I burst into Nothingness,
That slot in time where only pure
Spirit extends, absent and sure.

I am that spirit that denies,
High Priest of Laymen, Prince of Lies.
Your house is founded on my rock;
Truth crows; now I deny my cock.
Jock of this walk, I turn down all,
Robbing my Peter to play Paul.

I give up all goods I possess
To build my faith on faithlessness.
Black Peter, I belie my Lord --
You've got to die to spread the Word.
Now the last act; there's no sequel.
Soon, once more, all things shall be equal.

MAGDA GOEBBELS

-- 22 April, 1945.

(On this date, Magda and her six
children moved into the upper level
of the bunker.)

i

Who could dare to stay constant to
The sort who kept their faith to me?
　They hang on; they need help from you.
Who could dare to stay constant to
　Those less-than-no-help getting through?
　What use could some such weaklings be?
Who could dare to stay constant to
The sort who kept their faith to me?

ii

Who could you give devotion to
But those who treat you faithlessly?
　On all sides, this world threatens you;
Who could you give devotion to? --
　The strong, who don't care what they do,
　Overstep all bounds, then go free.
Who could you give devotion to
But those who treat you faithlessly?

iii

You raise a child devotedly;
He grows strong, goes off his own way.
　How helpless you must seem to be.
You raise a child devotedly
　And that shows him you need him; he
　Sees little reason not to stray.
You raise a child devotedly;
He grows strong, goes off his own way.

iv

What can you do but turn away
To show you're strong; then they'll stay true.
　Knowing how much loyalties pay
What can you do but turn away
　So that they'll need you. Now they'll stay
　Too scared to break their ties with you.
What can you do but turn away
To show you're strong; then they'll stay true.

EVA BRAUN

-- 22 April, 1945.

(Hitler's mistress received no public recognition and often felt badly neglected. Her small revenges included singing American songs, her favorite being "Tea for Two." Having chosen to die with him in the bunker, she appeared quite serene during the last days.)

Tea for two
And two for tea

I ought to feel ashamed
Feeling such joy. Behaving like a spoiled child!
So fulfilled. This is a very serious matter.
All of them have come here to die. And they grieve.
I have come here to die. If this is dying,
Why else did I ever live?

Me for you
And you for me

We ought never to flaunt our good luck
In the face of anyone less fortunate --
These live fools mourning already
For their own deaths; these dead fools
Who believe they can go on living . . .

And you for me
Alone.

Who out of all of them, officers, ministers,
These liars that despise me, these empty
Women that envy me -- so they hate me --
Who else of them dares to disobey Him
As I dared? I have defied Him to His face
And He has honored me.

We will raise
A family

They sneer at me -- at my worrying about
Frau Goebbels' children, that I make fairytales
For them, that we play at war. Is our war
More lost if I console these poor trapped rabbits?
These children He would not give me . . .

A boy for you
A girl for me

They sneer that I should bring
Fine furniture down this dank hole. Speer
Built this bed for me. Where I have slept
Beside our Chief. Who else should have it?
My furs, my best dress to my little sister --
They would sneer even at this; yet
What else can I give her?

Can't you see
How happy we would be?

Or to the baby
She will bear Fegelein? Lechering dolt!
Well, I have given her her wedding
As if it was my own. And she will have
My diamonds, my watch. The little things you
Count on, things that see you through your
Missing life, the life that stood you up.

Nobody near us
To see us or hear us

I have it all. They are all gone, the others --
The Valkyrie; and the old rich bitch Bechstein;
Geli above all. No, the screaming mobs above all.
They are all gone now; He has left them all.
No one but me and the love-struck secretaries --
Traudl, Daran -- who gave up years ago.

No friends or relations
On weekend vacations

That I, I above all, am chosen -- even I
Must find that strange. I who was always
Disobedient, rebellious -- smoked in the dining car,
Wore rouge whenever he said I shouldn't.
When he ordered that poor Chancellor Schussnig
Was to starve, I sent in food.

We won't have it known, dear,
That we own a telephone, dear.

I who joined the Party, I who took Him
For my lover just to spite my old stiff father --
Den Alten Fritz! -- and those stupid nuns.
I ran my teachers crazy, and my mother -- I
Held out even when she stuck my head in water.
He shall have none but me.

Day will break
And you will wake

We cannot make it through another month;
We follow the battles now on a subway map.
Even if the Russians pulled back --
His hand trembles, the whole left side
Staggers. His marvellous eyes are failing.
We go out to the sunlight less each day. We live
Like flies sucked up in a sweeper bag.

And start to bake
  A sugar cake

He forbade me to leave Berchtesgaden,
Forbade me to come here. I tricked
My keepers, stole my own car, my driver Jung.
He tried to scold me; He was too
Proud of me. Today He ordered me to leave,
To go back to the mountain. I refused.
I have refused to save my own life and He,
In public, He kissed me on the mouth.

For me to take
For all the boys to see.

Once more I have won, won out over Him
Who spoke one word and whole populations vanished.
Until today, in public, we were good friends.
He is mine. No doubt
I did only what He wanted; no doubt
I should resent that. In the face
Of such fulfillment? In the face
Of so much joy?

Picture you
Upon my knee;
Tea for two
And two for tea ...

ALBERT SPEER

-- 23 April, 1945.

(Berlin is almost encircled. Flying with Lt. Col. von Poser in two Storks, Speer lands on Unter den Linden near the Brandenburg Gate and hails an army truck to take him to the bunker.)

As we
Flew in,
The city like
Something out of
Dante -- a City of Dis.
Smoke rolling up, whole blocks
Burned out, walls broken in like
Paper boxes, cracked like egg shells;
The Reichstag, the Kaiser Wilhelm Church,
In ruins, charred. Out near Kyritz, refugees
Jamming the highways, families with carts, women
Hacking at a dead horse.

*(gets out of the truck on Voss Strasse where he
passes the bodies of deserters hung on streetlamps)*

He is
Ordering
More gun squads
Onto our own streets
For our own men; Germans
Hanging from their lampposts
Like venison in shops. No; my
Lamps, designed for Unter den Linden,
For his triumph. Their crime: they saw
No reason any more to die. Is this disloyal,
To care about this life? Can no one get enough
Of other people's dying?

Well?
Should we
Believe in our
Enemies' propaganda?
Bodies stacked like wood,
Jews herded into sealed rooms,
Strangled, shot, poisoned by gas,
Mass graves, incinerators day and night,
Medical experiments, lampshades of men's skin,
Rooms of women's hair, false teeth? Too absurd
To think of. How could the world not know? Merely
The stench of bodies burning . . .

>   *(in the garden he encounters the chimney*
>   *above the bunker's air shaft)*

Why
Let him
Live? Why
Let him breathe
One day more, filling
The air we breathe with smoke,
With his death's contagion? "If
Thine eye offend thee, pluck it out."

>   Who'll hang *us* to these lampposts?
>   Can nothing make them see?

I tried once, tried to slip that same gas
Into this air shaft that he takes his breath by.
Why fail? But I could as well cut off my right arm
With my left. Still, this withered limb, this contaminated . .

>   I could not reach Kattowitz.
>   I steered my own car into an
>   army truck's grill. Searing light.
>   Three months' convalescence.
>   Some kind Fate saved me, after all.

42

I let him live, as he has
let me live.
No doubt but each
is sick to dying
of each other.
I even keep his photograph
he gave me for *my* birthday
on my own desk
under Käthe Kollwitz' guillotine.

And yet his single purpose . . .

How much
Can any person
Hope to know that?
We know how much any
Man knows that he knows . . .

We must keep faith with that.

Until the Russians come . . .

(enters the bunker)

LT. GEN. HELMUTH "CRUSHER KARL" WEIDLING COMMANDER, 56th PANZER CORPS

-- 23 April, 1945.

(Weidling commanded the vital Seelow region. Condemned to death on April 22 because of false rumors, he cleared his name the next day and was appointed Commandant of Berlin. Here, he leaves the Führer's office.)

Why can't I learn: shut your yap; choke
Down the bag of shit they hand you?
Hot off the lines, sentenced to death,
I stormed down here: "What's going on
And why is this I'm to get shot?"
The Führer clutched my hand, named me
Commandant of this whole garbage dump,
Thousands of old women, little girls.
We'll screw the Slavs to death before
We slow them down. If I squeak through,
I can go in chains to Moscow, Lubianka,
The garottes and thumbscrews. In human charity,
Who'll give me one lead slug in the head?

ALBERT SPEER

-- 24 April, 1945.

(Having confessed his failure to carry out the most destructive orders, Speer bid Hitler and the others farewell, then left for the last time. He pauses in the damaged Chancellery which he had designed for Hitler.)

Not even
a farewell. Not even
one kind word for
my family. Cold
as his handshake.

The Thousand Year Reich! We didn't even
make good ruins. Charred
timbers; armchairs scattered; table legs sticking
though the wreckage; a broken wheel;
the skylight broken in. . .

The gallery 480 feet long; twice
the Hall of Mirrors at Versailles.
725 feet of polished marble floor
led to the Führer's reception hall.
The doors of marble 17 feet tall.
Window niches after Fountainbleu.

My father warned me: You have all
said goodbye to your senses. And
my professor:
Do you think you have created
something? It's showy; that's all.
Megalomaniac.
Losing all proportion. We would have had
to pull it down even without the shelling.
Like stumbling over some frozen mastodon,
some prehistoric sea beast. You ask
What lived here? These passageways --
Did blood pass here? Digestion?
Did this know love, ambition, fear?

Galileo noted that Nature cannot grow
a tree or build an animal beyond a certain
size. It falls apart of its own weight;
or else turns clumsy, monstrous . . .

Still
I was the
Largest boy in
School which spared me
Many a thrashing.

Still
With what
Joy we gave
Ourselves to these
Designs, to the headlong
Months of building, drawing,
Matching up materials. We built
This in eleven months. Eleven months.
That was impossible. We had two days over.

> . . . their greatest monuments of fame,
> And strength, and art are easily
> Outdone by spirits reprobate, and in
> An hour, what in an age they, with
> Incessant toil and hands innumerable,
> Scarce perform.

4500 workers in two shifts
2300 more throughout the Reich

Still
We were
Like gods; we
Did the things men
Cannot do. We did things
We could not do. We knew no
Limit. The factories were running,
The Reichsmark sound. We won our lands
Back; we could lift up our heads in Europe.

> Sublime spirit, you gave me,
> gave me all I asked.

He said:
The Impossible
Always succeeds. I
Feel it still there, still
Hovering above my shoulders like
A host of angels, that ghostly providence
We planned, that benison . . .

                The great chandelier
            cranked down to the floor,
                    its lusters crackling underfoot.
        That brilliance gone out.

Nov. 10: The Krystal Nacht in Berlin.
The glass of Jewish shop-fronts glitters
in the public streets and gutters.
The synagogues are still smouldering.

                        Such heaps of broken glass you'd think
                        The inner dome of heaven had fallen.

            Would
            You have me
            Go on building
            Nothing? My father --
            Even he, could he resist
            The chance to build so much?
            At Nuremberg, my Cathedral of Ice,
            Its pillars built from searchlights . . .

160 searchlights placed at intervals
of 40 feet. Visible to 25,000 feet
where they merge to a general glow.

        July 1: The execution of Ernst Roehm.
        March 5: The "Commissar Decree."

            Yes,
        we did what humans
            could not do. We passed
                all limit.

                        Oh I'll leap up to my
                        God! Who pulls me down?

        Only two weeks ago, we sat together over
        the models of Berlin, the plans for Linz . . .

                        And Goethe notes: it is provided for
                        that trees do not sprout into the Heavens.

    Now the searchlights sweep right, sweep left.

        In such a Spring as this, the thin ice
            in the mind

                        47

                    the skaters
            banking, gliding over
      the clear face of the abyss
          a few more hours.

                              O lente, lente currite,
                              noctis equi!

            You win and win until you can't
            win any more. The provinces revolt,
            the cells turn traitorous, each building
            its own way, beyond all limit, all
            reasonable design. Treachery becomes
            a way of life. We call it freedom.

      The healthy organism grows not in
      accordance with its past, with what
      has been done to it, but in accordance
      with the future, what it should become.

                  A few more hours and he
                        is gone. Suicide. One more
                  betrayal. Some will go
                        to the firing squads; some to
                              prison like a
                  cancer ward or a
                              cocoon.

            No more cathedrals, reception halls.
            Now it is a simple matter of how
            the poor survivors of this week
            can make it through the year.

                        Sometimes, I would leave my parents' formal
                        parlor with its glittering chandeliers,
                        its sham fireplace, and slip down to
                        play with the porter's daughter, Frieda.
                        The spare, simple quarters of a crowded,
                        close-knit family . . .

      It will be enough to build tin shacks
      to get them through next winter.

                  How will my wife, my unshaken
            wife, survive? I have seen
                        too little of my children . . .

                              48

MAGDA GOEBBELS

-- 27 April, 1945.

(On this date, Hitler gave Magda his golden party badge. Here, she contrasts herself with Gen. Paulus, whose Seventh Army fell at Stalingrad.)

I wear His badge, here, on my breast today;
    All those lost years, He must have wanted me.
I've borne old sacrifices; I obey
    Who stand restored: His heir, His deputy.

In this delirium of treachery
    On all sides, when our gods have turned away,
After the times He's scorned my company,
    I wear His badge, here, on my breast today.

Others have had His time, His gifts -- but they,
    When He called on them, failed Him wretchedly.
No Knights' Cross shines like this pin I display.
    All those lost years He must have wanted me.

Paulus was named Field Marshal, although he
    Lost Stalingrad -- we still had hopes they'd stay
To the last men, die for Him gloriously.
    I've born old sacrifices; I obey.

Paulus; we should have known that he'd betray
    And give up his men to captivity.
No false pity can make me flinch that way
    Who stand restored: His heir, His deputy,

Though I'm their keeper, too. I can't help see
    Their eyes wavering toward me while they play.
Sometimes I still break down. How can it be
    This is the breast that fed them? Yet today
        I wear His badge.

MARTIN BORMANN

-- 28 April, 1945.

(Despite long working hours, Bormann managed to write lengthy sentimental letters to his wife, sometimes twice a day. Here, he composes a letter while pondering his political situation: Himmler's betrayal leaves him in control of Germany just when he and it may both be lost.)

Dearly beloved Mommy-Girl,
    You have made me and my life rich . . . richer than Rockefeller and Morgan and all the millionaires at once.

> Mine. One more in the bag. Not one
> Dares squirm unless I say so.
>   Brandt. Göring. Himmler.

I am so happy we've had all nine children.

> The Chief: just like a fly-tape.
> Sprawled on their backs, their wings
>   Stuck in the gold slime.

By myself, I can't love you enough.

> Their legs twitch in the sunlight
> Like young girls screwing. They hum,
>   Hum softly, till they die.

All ten must join together so we can respond right.

> Today, we kissoff "Onkle Heinrich."
> Such flat treachery, I didn't need
>   To slip in my opinion.

Do give my best to "M." Though she's inferior to you, I'm still glad my will and passion overpowered her.

> What more could I have hoped for when
> I shoved through his new appointment:
>   Full Commander-in-Chief

Well, I *have* been a horrible wild ruffian!

> Over Army Group Vistula.
> Where that fidgeting idiot guaranteed
>   Defeat and his own disgrace.

Too bad, though, she failed to get pregnant by me. Coming from old Party stock, you could help her raise it right.

> And that blockhead thanked me for the post!
> Besides, the Eastern front kept
>   His nose out of Berlin.

Just like me, your only thought is our nation's destiny; "M" just worries about her family and friends.

> Goebbels and Speer remain, now --
> Neither, unfortunately, incompetent.
>   Yet Goebbels won't take power;

You dear, silly Momsy, how could you feel jealous of a girl like that!

> He'll kill himself. And Comrade Speer
> Botched his chances: he tried to save
>   The whole thing for himself.

No wonder I'm sick of politics; I've known too much ugliness, ineptitude, slander, distortion . . .

> My enemies drop like leeches; the Reich
> Slips into my grasp, just when the Chief
>   Will have to bow out.

nauseating false flattery, toadying, folly, idiocy, ambition, vanity, greed, etc., etc.

> Plainly I can't take his place.
> The Army's in disgrace. Who remains
>   So strong he could save

When can I retire, dearest Moms, and devote my life to my family, my library, and the commonsense prudent lives of cabbages and cabbage butterflies? Still, duty calls . . .

> Some few acres in negotiation?
> But someone weak enough
>   He'd still take our advice?

Never forget to warn the children:
  1. Never play with fire or matches.

        Like sailors starving in their lifeboat
        Who clubbed all other swimmers off,
          Drifting with no food, days,

  2. Never jump in the water when you're hot.

        Days, until the other had the sense
        To die. You've got the body. Then find out
          The bastard died with cholera . . .

  3. If someone offers candy to go along with them, always scream
     at once.

        There's always dull, dumb Doenitz --
        A friend, the Party's tool; he'd hear
          Sound practical experience.

  4. By no means always tell the truth -- unless events make it
     really necessary.

        The trick: transfer all power to him,
        Keeping him trussed up, hand and foot.
          Possibly handpick his cabinet,

Yet in all our trials, we have one consolation:

        Present them to him, in the Chief's voice,
        Part of his testament? Myself, possibly,
          As the Party Minister?

    Who is our first and our last?
    Who is our sacred treasure?
    Who is our everything best?
    Who is our gladsome pleasure?
Daddy and all nine children: Our Mommy!

        The trick: to present this to the Chief.
        The trick: to persuade the Chief he
          First presented this to us.

And do keep a close eye on young Eicke. She will be in contact with
our soldiers; you know where *that* can lead!

Then lay back under the Chief's
Shadow, where the live wires cross,
The phones, cables, radio --

Final victory must be ours -- otherwise, as you've said, the order of
the universe would be upset.

Keep his voice humming on the lines,
Feel out what powers tremble in the network,
Till that last, worst moment when

Yet if, like the old Nibelungs, we are doomed, we shall go to our deaths
proudly, with heads held high.

We've got to come up under the lights,
The guns, scurrying across the clearing
To a steadier obscurity.

Keep well and strong, Mommy mine. I know you are stalwart and will
raise the children by sound principles. Therefore I am wholly and
totally

Ever Thine,

M.

HERMANN FEGELEIN

-- 29 April, 1945; 0200 hours.

(Gretl Braun's husband was noted for lechery. On April 28, about to flee Berlin with an actress, he was arrested, demoted and jailed. When it was learned that Himmler had tried to contact the enemy, Fegelein -- his adjutant to the bunker -- was questioned, then led out and shot.)

[sweet jesus bleeding asshole no they cant
just shoot me   and three days ago I had
this sick world by the short hair   can they
my own men]
              in the guards station
singing   against regulations
whats more smoking
              [and with no trial
my own brotherinlaw   shit then
my wifes sisters husband   shit then
lover   an ss general   at only 37
blue eyes   blonde   superior physique
besides he told us we could leave   so
we all swore to stay and die while
we worked out ways]
              common soldiers
puking in the passage where the chief
takes meals
              [first run on all the snatch
down here   my stupid wife to put a
good word to the chief   besides
an ss general   shit then former
rates the ss court   which takes months
they all made their plans   shit
our golden pheasants   theyre who ought
to be here getting shot]
              the bad phonograph
broke into the medical supplies or else
the officers good wine

54

                                    [now this was down
the hole I had carlotta   damn well good
as anything of goebbels   and enough
swiss coin pinched out so we could buy in
on the best lake there   shit once hes
good and dead shit whod know me   37
retired and respectable]
                                    screwing her
while theyre dancing in the same room
that isnt done
                         [by now evas heard
about carlotta but she ought to care
about her little sister   say she put
a good word to   no   he as good as said
pump all we could   the best stock
blue eyed   blonde]
                                    spreadeagled in
the hall with her pants off   radio girl
I could have had her anytime I wanted
shit
      [three days ago when I said shit
they squat   say this was a test
at the last minute the reprieve
no]
      another gun squad off of whore patrol
thats no bad piece between them   altman
and schuler
                         [say I ordered them to
save me   no]
                              theyre leading me out
the other way   shit better ankles
on a cart horse
                              [say martin   reichsleiter
bormann   my best drinking buddy   say
he put in   no]
                         staring at me like
some numbskull serb
                              [martin came in
to finger me   said I was with himmler
in some sellout to the west   I wish
to sweet shit Id of known]

                              55

                              but I screwed them
every one   shit not that blackhaired slut
on the sofa   margaret   cocktease
turned me down
                          [theyll leave me   where
and come back in to bang these cunts
it will be all the same   who even keeps
the names]
                      now shes getting hers   no
and not that fat one in the dentist chair
I never screwed one even once   not
in a dentist chair
                      [leave it to himmler
hed weasel out   after I sold him
my own boss to martin   martin   his word
fixed my ass]
                      ivan will burn you out
like pissants   shed have been rotten
anyway   its only hours   woman come
                                                [after
my loyal service to the chief   the jews
the slovak gangs   the july assassins
I sent them to the meat hooks]
                                  which is
gods mercy to what ivans got saved up
for you   coming up now in the garden
youll bleed like virgins
                          [at least
I get mine from an ss squad   say Ive got
this pregnant wife   no]
                              so warm it up
for ivan
              [but it isnt fair   Im almost
his brother   shit almost   I as good
as crucified whole regiments   for him
him]
          oh youll just pray for vaseline
[sweet jesus no   they cant just
can they
          shit   shit   shit

COL. GEN. GOTTHARD HEINRICI
FORMER COMMANDER, ARMY GROUP VISTULA

-- 30 April, 1945.

(On April 28th, Heinrici counter-
manded Hitler's orders and com-
manded Manteuffel's Third Panzer
Army to retreat. He was relieved
of command and, on the 30th, ordered
back to Ploen. To keep him from
going back, a junior officer revealed
the facts of Rommel's death.)

For days I asked, I begged permission
To pull back and save our men. Denied.
Twice I offered to resign, take a rifle
In the front line trenches. Denied.
Now I have broken my oath, ordered
Manteuffel back out of encirclement.
So I, too, get orders: back to Ploen.
Rommel, I find only now, was not killed
At the front. Put to death by his own
Superiors. Superiors? Denied. Commanders.
By *my* commanders. For years I've sworn
The enemy more numerous than we thought;
I overlooked how many were behind me.
Manteuffel ordered guards for me. Which I
Declined: I take my way. To Ploen? Obedience
Remains my habit. What's more, now, two days . . .
And I remain master of the slow retreat;
It costs less lives.

EVA ♭ HITLER, geb. BRAUN

-- 30 April, 1945.

*(After her improvised civil wedding
and the brief reception, Eva sits on
the bed in her room alone. Hitler has
gone with Traudl Junge, his secre-
tary, to dictate his will before their
mutual deaths in a few hours. Frag-
ments of the Mass and the formal
Catholic marriage service run
through her mind.)*

Consummatum est.

It is accomplishèd.
    My mother's will be done.
                Is done.

        The Dodd Girl, the Valkyrie,
    Ley's wife, Geli above all --
            how many died
so I could carry her
    His name. When we were kids
        we looked at the eclipse
through snapshot negatives. They held
    their longing up to Him; their sight
            flashed out. Twice
    I tried to kill myself.

                *To Thee do we cry, poor banished
                    children of Eve.*

At the photographer's I called Him
        "Herr Wolf;" we met
            disguised. Later,
    He'd slip me an envelope
with enough to live on. Never
    a love note; never a word
        in public. I sat at my dresser
kissing His picture through glass;
        in April weather, the sun
            outside my windows
    sneered at me. We drove
to the Munich Station; His train

had gone; all we saw
was tail lights. He
was never there. Only my first "suicide"
brought Him in. Tonight
the third. This one
for dead sure.

What God hath joined together
let no man put asunder.

A boy, He wouldn't listen
to the priest; they'd find Him
catching sunlight
in a pocket mirror, playing it
around the trees, the courtyard. Even now
He has gone off with Traudl
to dictate His will. Since He cannot
have His will. He leaves me
this concession
I once was:
my crossed out name, my
new name on a piece of paper:
Eva ß Hitler, geb. Braun.

Therefore shall a man leave father
and mother and cleave to his wife.
They shall be one flesh.

And even if He came, He
would be missing; He
would not hear me; I
could look through Him
like a worn-out lantern slide. The priest
held up the monstrance
they said held the Host
before the people, right and left,
while we cast down our eyes. But I
crept up in the empty chapel,
one day, to the holy case. There
the sacred vestments, the gold
chains, the monstrance
rayed out gleaming
like the May sun. And in the
center, the tiny glass bead,
I could see nothing.
Nothing.

And yet I have these albums, these
pictures proving it all so.
We danced together; we
sat together over tea; even
the wedding ceremony . . .
My grandmother's brocade --
I left it at the mountain;
I had to wear my long black taffeta.
This ring delivered for me
by the Gestapo . . .

I am black but beautiful
ye daughters of Jerusalem.

With this ring I thee wed;
This gold and silver I thee bring.

. . . this ring torn off some Jew's hand.

in templo sancto tuo in Jerusalem.

I am the Black Bride that will be
devoured, that will pass
down into Him like used water
down a drain, a film stuck,
burning through, or reeling
back into itself.
Like all the women, all
the foreigners, our beautiful
young men -- all small
as red ants under
the magnifying glass
He reads His maps by.

Consummatum est.

To be so soon consumed and
never consummated.

O Thou who hast created
all things out of nothing . . .

Now each one has the nothing
they fought for. We have earned
our deaths. And yet,
my mother, not even she
would will me this. She only wants
it all to mean
her meaning. Something instead
of life. To tell the neighbors.
And that I give her. She
can rest.

Ite. Missa est.

My mother's will be mine.
Is
mine.

It is accomplishèd.

ADOLF HITLER

-- 30 April, 1945; 1520 hours.

*(Russian troops are in Voss and
Wilhelm Strasse. Hitler and Eva
have withdrawn to his sitting room;
she has already committed suicide.)*

More than fifty millions. More
Who killed that much; who else?

Russian: twenty million.
Jew: seven million, five hundred thousand.

"Casualties can never be high enough.
They are the seeds of future heroism."

All that and what good: what does
That save you? On and on and on . . .

Traitors on every side! Lies! Lies!

One gift, finally, to my faithful:
At Attila's bier. Last night,
My secretaries, cook, the short-wave girls.
More potent than bull-sperm; one cartridge
Each. A helping hand, to save you
From these Mongolians' greasy hands,
Pricks, the stink of jism. What then?
Some will sneak off West; some
Wait till the Russian tanks . . . overcome
By their own lust . . .

"Betrayed! Betrayed! Shamefully betrayed!
Deceit! Deceit! Lying past all revenge!"

Pole: three million.

"Casualties? But that's what
the young men are there for."

And seven at one blow.

Again last night, our movie:
Witzleben. General Joke Life. Choke Alive.
Shrivelled-up rat, hauled up, wriggling
On the meat-hook, handcuffed, naked,
Six times to choke and strangle. Five times
Hauled down. Brought back. Couldn't
Beg even to die. Not even. Scrawny
Pizzle wouldn't come again. Not dust.
He couldn't even . . .

> I bring you not peace but
> a sword. This death in honor.

> Gypsy: four hundred . . . four . . .
> four hundred thousand.

> Not one truly grateful.

> French: five hundred thousand.

Shovelling lime in a latrine. Oh,
It's dragon seed. We played it three times;
No satisfaction. Not even . . .

> Jugoslav: five hundred . . .

What use are facts, statistics?
The Impossible always succeeds.
Will enough and the lie turns true.

> German: spineless worms. Only four . . .
> four hundred . . . only four . . .

(turns to Eva's body)

Not even this one. Not even then.
She chose. Not watching her. Even
To come here was insulting. Mortal.

"Once recognized, the Grail Knight must be gone."

Betrayed to! Lies! Betrayed to!

Never to need anyone alive. Whose
Death gets you through? Whose death
Shows you more fit to live? Whose . . .

> Who's afraid of the big bad wolf,
>   Ha-ha-ha-ha-ha!

Tell me I have to die, then. Tell me.
What have I counted on? Tell me
The odds against me. You can't be
Sure enough. My name. My name on
Every calendar. Relentless, each year,
Your birth comes around. My death:
My lackey; my lickass general. My Will
Scrubs it all out, all of you, all gone . . .

> "I go with the precision and
> security of a sleepwalker."

I pick my time, my place. I take
This capsule tight between my teeth . . .
Set this steel cold against my jaw . . .
Clench, clench . . . and once more I
Am winning,
            winning,
                        winning . . .

DR. JOSEPH GOEBBELS

-- 1 May, 1945; 1800 hours.

*(The day after Hitler's death, Goebbels
and his wife climbed the steps into
the garden where both committed
suicide.)*

Say goodbye to the help, the ranks
Of Stalin-bait. Give too much thanks
To Naumann -- Magda's lover: we
Thank him for *all* his loyalty.
Schwaegermann; Rach. After a while
Turn back to them with a sad smile:
We'll save them trouble -- no one cares
Just now to carry us upstairs.

Turn away; check your manicure;
Pull on your gloves. Take time; make sure
The hat brim curves though the hat's straight.
Give her your arm. Let the fools wait;
They act like they've someplace to go.
Take the stairs, now. Self-control. Slow.
A slight limp; just enough to see,
Pass on, and infect history.

The rest is silence. Left like sperm
In a stranger's gut, waiting its term,
Each thought, each step lies; the roots spread.
They'll believe in us when we're dead.
When we took "Red Berlin" we found
We always worked best underground.
So; the vile body turns to spirit
That speaks soundlessly. They'll hear it.

AFTERWORD

A reader unfamiliar with the history of World War II may find many details in these poems outrageous, silly, monstrous, downright incredible. Yet it is precisely those details, not the more easily acceptable ones, which are based on historical fact. Writers, of course, must try to be believable; events are under no such constraint. World War II, and especially the Nazi regime, strained everyone's capacity for impossible facts.

Eva Braun's favorite song *was* "Tea for Two;" she even made up German words for it. According to his butler, Hitler preferred "Who's Afraid of the Big, Bad Wolf" even to *Lohengrin* -- all the more astonishing since his nickname had always been "Wolf." Until late in the war, most of the top Nazis loved Disney cartoons; after that, Hitler himself preferred movies of the drawn-out torture and deaths of those who tried to kill him on July 20, 1944. There is another film, recently recovered, which records his sexual perversion; Eva Braun had it secretly filmed, fearing that he might abandon her. What perversion it records has not yet been revealed; however, Otto Strasser and other acquaintances of Hitler's, as well as the American Dr. Langer, assert that it *was* the perversion depicted here.

All the figures in this cycle were actually in the places, doing and saying pretty much the things these poems show. General Weidling was condemned to death one day, then appointed Commandant of Berlin the next. He did remark that he wished they'd shot him instead; just as he predicts here, he did fall into the Russians' hands, went to Lubianka prison and so "disappeared." Goebbels did rejoice in the general destruction of his native land, claiming it would clear away the corrupt older social order so that a beautiful new society could be built there. Hitler did say that the young soldiers' purpose in the lines was to become casualties and that casualties could never be too high. He also said that his greatest flaw as a ruler was that he was just too kindhearted.

Even in depicting their everyday activities, I have drawn heavily on the recorded words of these characters. Bormann did write long, slushy letters to his wife; his letter, here, is made entirely of quotes and paraphrases from the actual surviving letters. Many lines in Eva's poems, as in those of Goebbels', are quotations from their letters or recorded conversations. In brief, I have helped myself, whenever possible, to the facts. They are hard to improve upon.

At the same time, these poems sometimes depart from fact -- even from historical probability. In his April 18th poem, Albert Speer compares Hitler to a friend of his, a cancer specialist who died unknowing that he, himself, had cancer. That comparison was actually made by Speer during an interview with me in 1972; moreover, his friend had only recently died and was not named Paul. Again, it is not really likely that Fegelein actually passed through the bunker orgy on his way out to be shot on April 29; even if the orgy had started that early, he probably would have been led out some other way. Life has all a lifetime to reveal character; writers must be not only believable, but also comparatively brief.

As I see Hitler's early life, he *did* team up with his mother to drive his older half-brother, Alois, out of the house. This was, I think, the paradigm for many later manipulations and betrayals. It also seems to me that the death of his younger brother, Edmund, left much permanent warpage. There is, on the other hand, no evidence that Hitler ever stole Edmund's birthday cake or soiled the remainder, nor that his mother then made a cake only for the two of them. What the evidence *does* strongly suggest is that she badly spoiled him and encouraged him to oppose his father's discipline. I have tried to invent an example of such behavior which would gear with such historical evidence as Hitler's behavior while imprisoned at Landsberg Fortress, his later obsession with cake-eating, etc. This birthday cake episode, then, is a counter for actual but unrecorded events which, after the habit of actuality, may well have been less immediately graspable, less credible.

A similar substitution happens in Speer's poem dated April 24th. As he leaves the bunker, taking a last look at the ruins of the Chancellery he had built for Hitler, many literary quotations rise in his thoughts, projecting his sense of complicity and guilt. These quotations -- Marlowe, Milton, Whitehead, Frost -- are nearly all from English literature. Yet it is unlikely that Speer knew our literature so well at that time. I, on the other hand, don't know German literature well enough to produce quotations of the necessary resonance. Dealing with Goebbels or some of the other more consciously intellectual characters, I have been able to find appropriate passages from German literature. Speer demands something much less conscious, less obvious, less ready-to-hand. Once again, my English quotations are meant to be counters for the German passages which might occur to such a man in such a situation.

Finally, however, there is a much more important kind of divergence from recorded fact. In certain ways, the figures in these poems *do* differ from anything recorded about their historical counterparts. The "Dr. Goebbels" in my cycle has a playfulness and malevolent glee unlike anyone's recollection of the actual man. Very few, indeed, found him playful. The "Adolf Hitler" of these poems spouts neither praise and justification of himself, nor the endless mendacious accusations of others so typical of the historical Führer. Throughout the poems, he and the other characters are much more open and direct about their destructive feelings and intentions than their historical counterparts ever were.

This involves the poems' deeper intentions. There is no need, after all, to reveal what the Nazis did or said; an enormous body of research already reveals that in horrifying detail. The Nazis -- like some others one may have encountered -- often did or said things to disguise from the world, sometimes from themselves, their real actions and intentions. My aim is to investigate the thoughts and feelings behind the public facade which made those actions necessary or even possible. My poems, then, must include voices they would hide from others, even from themselves.

May, 1977

W. D. Snodgrass was born in Beaver Falls, Pennsylvania, in 1926 and was educated at Geneva College and the State University of Iowa. He has taught at Cornell University, the University of Rochester, Wayne State University and is currently Professor of English and Speech at Syracuse University.

A member of the National Institute of Arts and Letters and a Fellow of the Academy of American Poets, W. D. Snodgrass also has been the recipient of fellowships in poetry from the *Hudson Review* and from the John Simon Guggenheim Memorial Foundation. In 1960 W. D. Snodgrass was awarded the Pulitzer Prize for his first book of poems, *Heart's Needle*.